The Little Book of Garden Villains

Moreton Morrell Site

© Allan Shepherd 2006
The Centre for Alternative Technology Charity Ltd
Machynlleth, Powys SY20 9AZ
Tel. 01654 705980 Fax. 01654 702782
email. pubs@cat.org.uk web. www.cat.org.uk www.ecobooks.co.uk

Registered Charity No. 265239

ISBN 1 90217 532 8

1 2 3 4 5 6 7 8 9 10

Design: Graham Preston
Illustrations: Annika Lundqvist

Mail Order copies from: Buy Green By Mail, Tel. 01654 705959

The details are provided in good faith and believed to be correct at the time of writing, however no responsibility is taken for any errors. Our publications are updated regularly; please let us know of any amendments or additions which you think may be useful for future editions.

Text pages printed on 100% recycled paper.
Cover printed on Era Silk board; an FSC product which contains 50% recycled fibre by The Cambrian Printers Ltd., Aberystwyth. Tel. 01970 627111.

Front cover photograph: Meul/ARCO/naturepl.com

The Little Book of Garden Villains

by Allan Shepherd

illustrated by Annika Lundqvist

Foreword

I've been asked to write this foreword by Allan Shepherd, author of this irreverent and, I might add, rather timely little book on dealing with garden pests. I can't say that I agree with some of his more, how should I put this, um, pacifist ideas about dealing with pests, but he's an old friend of the family and one must support ones brethren – what, what. Where I do agree with him is that you can't be vigilant enough when it comes to dealing with garden villains. In the immortal words of that aptly occupied old Home Guard soldier Corporal Jones, the butcher, 'They don't like it up 'em.' Organisation, that's the key to sorting out your pest problems. I'm what Allan might call a commander type. But then you've probably guessed that already. According to him, when it comes to dealing with pests there are four main character types of gardeners – the commander, the soldier (or vigilante), the defender and the pacifist. I'll let him explain all about it later, so far as to say I gather my troops and let them do the work for me. Not that it always goes to plan. Sometimes I have to go over the top myself and do the dirty work. Old soldier I might be, but never too old to show them the cold steel. And then there's always a bit of pre-emptive defending to do… The odd copper ring to push back the marauding hoards of slugs trying to break over the ramparts of my fortress pots. What I am not is a pacifist… The type of gardener who leaves it all to nature. I will fight them on the beeches, as they say.

Anyway, that's enough from me. Chocks away and on with the show…

Kind regards,

Wing Commander Gravesny Throttle-Mite, (retired).

Acknowledgements

Many thanks to Annika Lundqvist for her fantastic illustrations and for making *The Little Book of Garden Villains* so much more fun. Thanks also to Caroline, Graham, Chloe, Hele, Fred and Christian for their support and varied contributions… And to Bethan for keeping me going with fun and laughter through the perturbations. Here's to a quick winter and a new spring. Much love to you all.

Contents

Part One

Don't Panic

What keeps you awake at night? The unpaid bills? Stress at work? Wayne Rooney's metatarsals? Or is it something more earthy.

The terrifying sound of an imaginary caterpillar cutting through the green blooded veins of a cabbage leaf perhaps. The thought of the halloween radula of a slug, with its thousands of tiny Dracula-tooth-like protrusions, munching its way round the crisp tender edges of your freshly planted lettuce seedlings. Maybe it's the charming yet merciless rabbit, a living nightmare of Plasticine persecution – if only there was a real Wallace and Gromit in every neighbourhood!

Pests – loathe them or really, really loathe them, they're here to stay, bringing gardeners something to sweat about. Well, gardening would just be too peaceful without them, wouldn't it. As soon as you become a gardener you enter the twilight zone where murder becomes mundane.

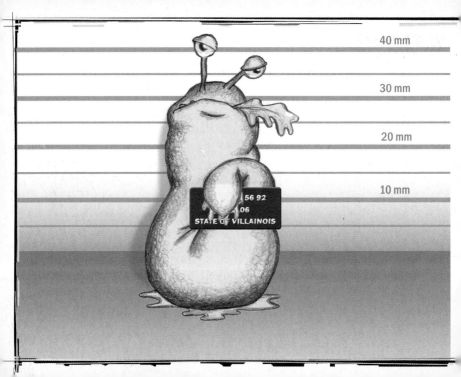

The Slug

Wanted – for crimes against vegetables.

Sucker or feeder – feeder.

Favourite meal – newly planted seedlings with weak defences, though its tastes are not confined to the young, nor for that matter to the living. They love composting. Have even been known to eat their dead relatives.

Where to look – during the night and in very humid and wet conditions you'll find them all over vegetables, soft fruit, flowers, on top of the leaves, underneath the leaves, climbing up the stems, slime-ing their way between plants. During the day in dry conditions you'll find them hiding in cracks and crevices, patches of weeds, under rocks and bits of wood. Some live underground. Some on the surface.

Evidence – slime trails, holes, magical disappearing plants.

How to stop them – regular hoeing will break up slime trails, disturb resting slugs and destroy eggs. Remove possible hiding places (especially patches of weeds), use beer or pheromone traps, put down barriers, encourage predators such as frogs, hedgehogs, Indian runner ducks.

Biological control – Nemaslug®.

Vegetarian gardeners beware, your principles will be challenged.

But all gardeners are different. No two feel the same about the persecution of pests. Some will kill slugs but not mice. Some mice but not slugs. Some will squash aphids between finger and thumb. Others will water cannon them into oblivion. Some will spray them with chemicals – but we're not going to talk about such alien beings here.

If you've ever wondered at the depths to which people will sink to get rid of their foes then read CAT's *The Little Book of Slugs*, a litany of torture to offend and beguile. Slugs are frozen, burnt, trodden on, thrown under the wheels of motor cars, drowned in beer (though not held under by green fingers), cut with scissors, impaled with skewers, shrivelled with salt, blown up with bran, even suffocated in recycled plastic bags – which I guess has at least some semblance of the ecological. As it is for slugs, so it is for all of the unfortunate garden fauna branded with the stamp of villainy. Moles, ants, beetles, mites, scales, flys, thrips, grubs, butterflies, moths – the suckers, the munchers, the borers and miners – all meeting sticky ends because they have the bad luck to want our plants for themselves.

Why do we get so worked up about pests? Because pests steal the rewards of our labour. How many times has a gardener raised with tenderness and love a crop of seedlings in a tray, daintily pricking out each one, carefully planting them into the soil, only for all that love and caution to amount to nothing, because, on their first night out in the big bad world, they are swooped on by an army of slugs. No wonder we get vicious. No wonder the nation's gardens are filled at night with the searchlight beams of torches. Sweeping downward towards earth in great war-like arcs, over leaves and under them, too, for the enemy lurks in gravity defying places.

But there is also something fascinating about our foes. Something that brings out the biologist in us. Where do they go to hide when they've finished eating our plants? How do they mate? When do their children become adults? And while they're busy enjoying our plants, who enjoys them? What deadly creature is lying in wait to make them lunch, or even more gut churningly horrible, home…for this is what the parasitoids do. They occupy their hosts' bodies, feed on them from the inside out, keep them alive for just long enough to become fully functioning creatures themselves and then move on…deadly guests on a Grand Tour.

And if you're not fascinated by the facts of their lives you should be, for nothing is more useful to the gardener than information about how pests live. Take for example the usual suspects illustrated throughout this book by our 'garden police' artist Annika Lundqvist. The Royal Horticultural Society receives more enquiries about these pests than any others. If you can't find enough information to satisfy your quest for knowledge, dig a little deeper using the references in the Directory (page 111).

The lives of the great torturers – in which we gardeners are the tortured.

Pests torture gardeners, not the other way round. They haunt our gardens and betray our sensibilities. Normally sane people turn into rabid obsessives, their behaviour bordering on the compulsive. Once I killed a mouse with the back of a rake. From a standing start I flicked the rake up, brought it round over my head, in a beautiful arc of motion, which ended when the head of the rake collided with the head of the mouse, and bang... It was all over in two seconds. Afterwards I was ashamed. But at the time I have to say I was thrilled by the kill. The mouse was eating my precious pea seeds.

Some people take to counting how many pests they find in their garden. Mrs Whately recorded her burgeoning obsession with numbers in her contribution to *The Little Book of Slugs*: 'Last night I collected 588!!!

[her exclamation marks]. And since I started keeping a record, on 23rd May, I have bagged 2,358.' This little quote paints a picture of a gardener so in love with gardening that she is prepared to go out and pick literally hundreds of slugs off her plants in one night. If you've never picked up a slug with your bare hands you won't appreciate what a determined act of dedication this is.

Each slug is a little time bomb of slime waiting to explode in your grip. The minute you pick them up the stuff pours out of their pores and on to your hand. It's a defensive mechanism passed down through the aeons. You can scrub and scrub slime-sticky fingers till you think your skin will blister. It makes no difference. This stuff sticks longer than super-glue.

Some people like the feel of a pest between their fingers and will take bloody vengeance on anything unfortunate enough to end up there. Caterpillars, which we will quite happily encounter on a nature walk, are given no truck in a garden. Out in the fields we may marvel at their stripes and colours, the eye spots and glorious manes of hair Mohicaning down their backs. In the garden, where they appear like so many Vivienne Westwood models on the green catwalk of our leaves, we say, out loud sometimes, how dare they? We're 'disgusted of Tunbridge Wells'.

The heat rises to our necks, our faces redden. Our blood vessels threaten to burst. We feel like shouting blue murder, but we know that our neighbours are listening and, in our paranoia, feel that they are secretly hoping for disaster to befall us. So we remain quiet and stealthy. And squeeze on.

Others can't quite bring themselves to murder. Pests find themselves on trajectories they would never have thought possible. That go against evolutionary expectations… Have you ever seen a slug fly? But fly they do – with the greatest of ease. When hand propelled they are veritable slime javelins. Or caterpillars – furry spinning boomerangs that don't come back. Where are they headed? Wasteland? Roads? The next door neighbour's garden? Ponds? And those pests that don't fly are caged and carried out. Mice sit snug in humane traps and are driven away in 4x4s, or more ecologically, in the panniers of a bicycle. To find a new life in somebody else's neighbourhood. And perhaps to end it in someone else's trap.

And then there are those who try and be good, but whatever they do they just can't seem to get it right. Elva Davies for example: 'I was so angry at the state of the flowers being eaten alive, I went on a slug rampage. I'd collected a good amount but decided (being a vegetarian) I couldn't bring myself to kill them, so I put them on the bird table. Watching them slowly slime off, I thought they're not going to get the better of me! So I then poured salt all around the bird table, so they would have to stay and become bird food. I was horrified when they started to fizz, and realising what I'd done, quickly gathered them all in a bucket and tried to rinse the salt off with a hosepipe! NEVER AGAIN! I throw them on the garden waste pile now.'

Some people enlist the services of wildlife in more subtle ways. No hand feeding required! These gardeners are not mere foot soldiers but commanders. They devise strategies to establish regular armies of predators and set up the field of battle in their favour. They will not dirty their own hands unless it is absolutely necessary. In preference they will occasionally bring in a mercenary force for special jobs: parasitic wasps arrive through the post by special delivery, as if they have been called to assist by the first runner at Marathon. If there are armies of slugs the commander counters them with battalions of frogs, slow-worms and hedgehogs. They might even keep a couple of Indian Runner Ducks to peck away at the crevices for weed hidden gems. I've seen them march around raised beds like good soldiers – looking every bit as splendid as the guardsmen on Horse Guards Parade. If there are airborne divisions of incoming blackfly circling, commanders make sure a squadron of predators is ready for action – dragonflies and hoverflies, parasitic wasps, Tachinid flies, blue tits and thrushes. How do they do this? They fill their gardens with flowers and feeders, hedgerows and ponds. And let nature take its course.

There are many games to be played in a conflict and one gardener or another plays all of them. The defensive game is played by the gardener who believes in the Maginot Line. A barrier beyond which no pests will travel. He cannot stay his hand and leave it all to nature. His garden is littered with devices and gadgets, barriers and traps. Rattling milk tops, shiny CDs, green plastic netting, ultrasonic devices, sunken beer pools made out of yoghurt pots. The defender knows which pests can be brought to heel by such devices and is ingenuity itself when it comes to coming up with something new. He will ring pots with copper, ask his friends to save eggshells and upturn grapefruit halves on his soil to trap slugs; grease the trunks of fruit bushes and set up pheromone traps for moths. He will balance small pots stuffed with straw upside down on the end of a pole – just to catch earwigs.

It says much about who we are, the way we deal with pests. Are we organised? Do we fire-fight? Could we hurt a flea? Are we relaxed, up-tight, pro-active, reactive? Are we good at observing? Can we hold back and weigh up the seriousness of a situation or do we believe in blanket responses? Can we live with a little bit of damage or must everything be pristine? Do we need to change our attitude in the garden to do a better job? Are we commanders, soldiers, defenders or pacifists?

Know your enemy – what's the worst thing a pest can do?

Pests eat, suck, bore and mine their way into trouble. Not to mention scratch, tunnel, batter and urinate (if they're a fox) too. No part of a plant is sacred – leaves, flowers, stems and roots – there are pests for all parts of a plant and pests for most plants. Ironically, weeds seem to escape the attention of pests – some of them, such as Japanese knotweed, notoriously so. Japanese knotweed is one of those lucky plants that now finds itself lodged in a country far out of reach of its natural predators. Even sheep will demur faced with this particular free lunch.

But pests don't always destroy a plant. Sometimes they riddle the leaves with irritating bullet holes, or cannonball the edges into semi-circles. Such injuries are not as bad as they seem. A plant can carry a certain amount of damage, just as a ship will carry on moving forward with a few tears to the mainsail. But even then, you're never quite sure how bad the damage will get. The machine-gunner flea beetle, which leaves small holes all over the peppery leaves of oriental brassicas, rocket and radish, will fatally rat-a-tat-tat a young seedling if the infestation is severe. If it is not, then the seedling will survive happily enough albeit blemished.

So what's the worst a pest can do? Let's take each of the main pest types in order and assess the ferocity of their attack. I'll start with the suckers. There's one billion born every day…

The Suckers

No rhyming slang will bring forth an adequate expletive for the infuriation caused by the loss of a plant that has had the goodness sucked out of it. No innocuous leaf holes here. The stem of a plant falls like a piece of timber beneath the axe. With the life-giving sap that kept it up gone into the mouths of small needle mouthed insects, it wilts and droops. It takes a battalion of aphids, whitefly and red spider mites to finish a plant off. But in the invertebrate army, battalions are never in short supply.

Nor is the damage limited to stems. Leaves are attacked with equal vim and vigour, curling and distorting under duress. What goes in must come out and while they suck, aphids also poo (or at least excrete). The inaptly named honeydew that comes forth causes cosmetic damage to plants, as well as providing a sugar rich food source on which fungal moulds will thrive. And when they are done with one plant the suckers move on to the

2 mm

1.5 mm

1 mm

0.5 mm

00 227 5 7 778
9.17.06
STATE OF VILLAINOIS

Aphid

Wanted – for seditious sucking.

Sucker or feeder – sucker.

Favourite meal – likes to go out with a gang of mates to stems near leaf joints and leaves. Sucks the sap of plants like a kid devouring a milk shake. Loves nitrogen rich tips of plants at the start and end of the season in particular, so these are crucial times to spot them and do something.

Where to look – vegetables, flowers, fruit, even weeds and wildflowers are prone to attack. Look under stems and leaves. Look out for armies of ants going up and down trees or plants. They're protecting the aphids and they're taking it in turns to eat the honeydew they produce. Where the trail stops you'll find an aphid colony.

Evidence – plants with wilting tops and curling leaves, sticky honeydew.

How to stop them – encourage natural predators like ladybirds, lacewing, parastic wasps, hover-fly. Pinch them or jet them off plants with water. Biological control – Aphidius.

Organic pesticides – insecticidal soap, pyrethrum, rapeseed oil.

next, taking plant viruses with them, infecting new victims as they make their way around the garden.

Whether you're reading this book at Christmas or not, the average garden endures seven suckers sucking – shieldbugs, thrips, aphids, whitefly, mites, scale insects, and pysllids (which also appear in some reference books under the rather unhelpful common name of 'sucker'). Only the most disgruntled ex would send you a present of all seven on one day. Taken as a whole they can do considerable damage. Thankfully, as with any group of pests, the likelihood of being placed under siege by the seven seditious suckers all at the same time is fairly remote, though of course not technically impossible.

Of the seven, aphids are probably the most familiar and troublesome to the average gardener (see front cover in glorious Technicolor®). There are 4,000 known species of aphids worldwide and a big gang of them find their way into the garden. They are Class A suckers. Fast reproducers

– bypassing sex for multiple virgin births. And extremely prolific. Working their way across many plants in a season. None of which should take our attention away from the other six – each of whom can cause considerable damage given half a chance.

Finding suckers is not always easy – all, except some species of scale insects and the shieldbugs, being under 3mm long. Look out for conglomerations of tiny writhing bodies on the underside of a leaf. Thrips are an exception to this rule, they prefer to suck from the sunny side up. So, too, are scale insects, which stick to leaves like limpets, remaining immobile for most of their lives, gently sucking sap from beneath a waxy shell that looks a bit like one half of those flying saucer sweets you used to buy as a kid.

One last thing about suckers before we move on. Beware of guilt by association. Insects are always being tarred with the same brush, but careful gardeners learn to distinguish between the good and the bad. Not all mites are bad for plants. Many feed on fungal growth on rotting plants or on algae, and some are predators of pest insects and other mites. Make sure your mite is right.

The Feeders

Whereas suckers tend to concentrate on leaves and stems, feeders are a much more democratic bunch, including all parts of the plant in their menu plans. There are five regiments of feeders and although some pests may belong exclusively to one, this is not always the case. For ease of identification we can split them into root feeders, leaf feeders, stem feeders, flower feeders and fruit feeders. Some of the feeders are all too familiar and obvious – slugs and caterpillars, for example. Others are much harder to spot. Quite often the only evidence of their existence comes after the damage is done.

f a threat as their larvae (the
Of course they look wildly
s is a crucial skill. And
are caterpillars and look,
caterpillars, the larvae of
six legs, through sluggish

tween pest and predator so
might imagine. The larvae of
ing like as shiny and
me-shaped
ing from
aphids,
r

Root feeders are the undercover operatives of the pest world, just as fond of their vegetables as we are. Some of these pests are tiny, even in comparison to other pests. Microscopic nematodes (also called eelworms) feed on several of our favourite plants. Chrysanthemum, Narcissus, onion, Phlox and potato all have their own tailored eelworm that feeds within the host plant. There are many more that live in the soil and nibble on root hairs. What a specialised little existence that is! Not all nematodes are bad for plants. Many are predators – attacking other nematodes and many larger invertebrates, including other root feeders such as chafer grubs and vine weevil larvae. All root feeders, including cutworms (the caterpillars of some moths), wireworms, cabbage root fly larvae and carrot fly larvae, cause damage by eating or boring their way through roots, corns, bulbs and tubers. The damage restricts nutrient and water uptake, which in turn restricts growth and causes wilting.

By habit many of the other four battalions are easier to spot – munching

their way openly through stems, leaves, flowers and fruits. They in
Lepidoptera (moths and the cabbage white butterfly), Coleoptera (b
Diptera (flies), Molluscs (several species of slugs and snails), Hym
tera (wasps, ants and sawflies), Mammals (rabbits, moles, sheep an
on) and Birds. In short, quite a wide variety of the animal kingdom

Although distinguishing the difference between them, and the an
and variety of damage that can be caused by each and every one of
groups, sounds like a Sisyphean[1] task, in any one of these orders or
classes of species only a handful of individuals within the group co
called pests (even many of the slugs and snails don't make it throu
the status of garden villain). The rest are harmless or beneficial. Fo
species of beetle and fly that eats plants there are plenty of others t
pests.

[1. In Greek mythology Sisyphus was ordered to spend the afterlife pushing a rock up a hill even though l
would never reach the top. A Sisyphean challenge is interminable.]

This makes the adult beetles just as much
general name given to the young of insects).
different and learning to spot these differenc
whereas the larvae of all butterflies and mot
if not the same as each other, then at least li
beetles vary from fast-running predators wit
herbivores, right down to legless grubs.

It's important to recognise the difference b
we remove the real threat and not the one we
the ladybird (a predator not a pest) looks not
friendly as the adult form – the picturesque c
creature we all love. But in the process of tu
ugly ducklings to swans they eat hundreds o
and we need them just as much as their prett
parents.

Adult beetles also vary enormously, in size, shape, colour, weaponry speed, and style of movement. There are 4,000 species of beetles in Britain, and only 27 of these are regular garden pests. The rest are harmless or beneficial. You don't have to be Charles Darwin to appreciate their diversity. Fly, walk or swim, beetles are fab.

Beetles, moths and caterpillars are not the only species that work for both sides. We have an ambivalent attitude to wasps and birds too – all of which work away at undoing the positive image we should have of them as friends of the gardener. Wasps are universally hated by almost everyone from early childhood on and adult gardeners are no exception to the rule. Wasps are often blamed for inflicting damage on fruits but they are more likely to capitalise on damage caused by birds than inflict it themselves, unless the fruit is a soft-bodied over-ripe globe like a plum or grape. And

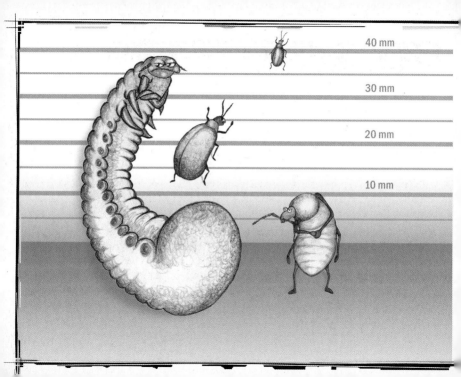

40 mm

30 mm

20 mm

10 mm

The Beetles: Chafer Grub, Red Lily Beetle, Flea Beetle, Vine Weevil

Wanted – for jailhouse rock.

Sucker or feeder – feeders.

Favourite meal – wide variety of plants.

Where to look – around the roots of plants, on the stems, around the leaves, on seed heads.

Evidence – in all species both the adults and the young eat various parts of the crop. The young tend to feed on roots and the adults on leaves. Root damage can lead to wilting, browning off and die-back. Attacks on leaves are evident when holes appear.

How to stop them - encourage a wide range of predators. Check plants regularly and if infestation is severe remove and kill any beetles found. The highly mobile flea beetle can be dislodged from leaves with a grease board trap (described in the 'Soldier' section). Keep cultivated areas free of weeds.

Biological control – in the case of the chafer grubs and vine weevil you can use the biological control Heterorhabditis megidis.

even these fruit-loving, stinging wasps have their uses. I'd often wondered what ants were afraid of. After witnessing one being air lifted off the ground by a wasp, I now know. Wasps are great predators.

Both ants and wasps (along with bees) are members of the Hymenoptera family of species but neither damages plants in the way a fourth member of the family does – the sawfly. Adult sawflies are not a problem but their larvae offspring are. They are leaf feeders, capable of causing widespread damage. Look out for them. They look like caterpillars but have more clasping pro-legs (at least seven compared to five or less for caterpillars). You'll know what a clasping pro-leg is when you see it. Caterpillars and larvae use them to hold on to branches and leaves as they move along. They look a bit like legs but are obviously different to the six real legs all insects have.

Birds make trouble for the gardener too, however much we love to encourage them with seeds and nuts. They will strip a bush of fruit without a second thought. They will tear strips off brassicas. They will pinch out flowering buds at the start of a season and steal seeds at the end. Yet they are also formidable predators, collecting endless caterpillars and grubs to raise their young (a pair of blue tits will forage over 10,000 to raise a brood).

Then there are those insects with which we are less familiar – the flies. We may know what a bluebottle looks like, or a house fly, but unless you're an entomologist or a keen gardener you won't be able to put faces to the names gall midge or leaf miner or even the more common carrot root fly. In all cases it is not the adult fly that you need to look out for, but the earthbound, unimpressive, charisma-free grub of an offspring, which does all the damage. Not that their habits are at all usual or uninteresting.

They each have a slightly different type of damage to offer. Take the gall makers for example. There are three types of gall makers: gall mites, gall wasps and gall midges. Only the gall midges are true flies, but they all do more or less the same type of damage to a plant. The infant maggots secrete a chemical on leaves or buds that forces the foliage to enclose them, wrapping them up like a snug maggot pasty. The resultant bump in the leaf is called a gall. The cheek of it… Most other fly maggots are leaf miners. They tunnel and eat, eat and tunnel. Eventually a whole network of engineered hollows can be seen as a pattern through the leaf. An expert eye can match each pattern to a particular pest.

The Accidentals

There are some pests that need no introduction, whose faces and names are all too familiar: slugs, snails, moles, rabbits. Even a child of two is familiar with each of these, although of course, with childhood innocence on their side, they are not pests at all but cutesie animals. Given the choice, which of the four would you say was the odd one out? Moley of course. Poor old mole is an accidental. A carnivore at a vegetarians' party. He is the Private Godfrey of the pest world – 'May I be excused?' Certainly not. For the mole has a unique role to play in the fury and thunder of the expletive-ridden world of the tormented gardener. He is the 'undertaker'. Plants sink inexorably downwards as he tunnels away at the foundations of vegetable plots. Turf blisters and pops on lawns as soil erupts its way to the surface. Bowling green lawns are bunkered with craters. Accident is no excuse under the law of pest control. And poor old Godfrey must run with the pack. As fast as his little legs will carry him.

There are other accidentals too: the fox, the dog and the cat. No plants eaten. Just seed beds scratched, bulbs dislodged, droppings dropped and lawns yellowed with urine. Each one exercises the gardener in its own peculiar fashion. Timers, sprays, alarms and ultrasonic devices plague suburban gardens with twitches, bleeps, ratcheting mechanisms and jets of wasted water, all to keep these garden wanderers at bay. Never mind that they catch mice, rats and rabbits, when unwanted they are still a pest.

There is one more accidental worth mentioning, though fearing the scorn of some gardeners I hesitate to call it such: the ant. Perhaps it is not a true accidental, but rarely does an ant dismantle a plant. Not like a slug, or an aphid, or a rabbit. An ant is a tunneller like the mole. But only to make a palace for his queen. The fine soil excavated to make room for the royal household appears in piles in lawns, like so much spilt egg-timer sand. Annoying perhaps but rarely damaging to plants, except for the odd one whose root ball is undermined by the work. Not a major crime in the garden then, and certainly accidental. In fact ants are decomposers by nature, mopping up the detritus of the garden, scurrying back and forth to their earthen kingdoms with hidden treasures from the rough and tumble, low down world of the soil bed. Here they forage amongst lost stems and petals for tiny scraps of plant life.

The ant has one questionable habit, though, that gets it into trouble with the gardener. Its quest for the mysteriously appealing honeydew. Or aphid excrement as the scatologist may wish to call it. Aphids suck more sap than they could possibly know what to do with, and that which they cannot digest comes out the other end as a sticky tonic for ants. Of course it is not designed specifically for ants, but ants make use of it, and aphids make use of the protection ants seem prepared to offer to defend their source of honeydew. Any predator that moves on an aphid protected by an ant will have to be prepared to do battle with the little stinger to get what it wants. An ant fights hard and can quickly summon friends to the cause so a colony of aphids have good reason to live with a little ass kissing. God or Darwin? Whatever you believe in, some occurrences are beyond explanation.

Aesthetic damage – does it matter?

Quite a lot of pest damage is aesthetic, meaning that it only harms our visual enjoyment of a plant, not the plant itself. Aesthetic values vary enormously from person to person. I'd recommend getting a pest reference book such as the RHS Encyclopedia of Pests and Diseases, or a general organic reference book like the HDRA Encyclopedia of Organic Gardening. Both books describe how much damage each individual pest causes and whether this damage is purely visual or injurious to the health of the plant. Some people get upset at the sight of the pests themselves, and can't stand to have them spoiling the look of the plants, whilst others really don't notice. The same is also true of pest control measures. At what point do they themselves become intrusive…? I would rather grow plants that slugs don't eat, than see my garden littered with blue slug pellets. Not only would the colour look completely unnatural, but the pellets would be a visual reminder of poison. And why would I want that in my garden? Likewise, too many traps and barriers in a garden make the space you create seem unduly industrialised and messy. There is a balance to be struck between the mess caused by pests and the mess that we ourselves create.

Flatworms

Flatworms are one of those accidental pests I haven't yet mentioned, because they don't cause damage to any plants in any direct way. However, they do eat earthworms, and all soils need a healthy population of worms. If soils don't have a healthy population of worms they become hard, compacted and difficult to drain, leading to waterlogging around the roots of plants. This causes plants to weaken. Flatworms are not native to this country and were brought here in imported soils, possibly in the rootballs of exotic plants. If you are buying plants check the rootballs for flatworms and signs of other pests, removing some of the compost to see what's going on. Flatworms are a few inches long, black and flattened (not round like native worms). If you find flatworms in a rootball you should remove and kill the ones you can see and then submerge the rootball in water over 30°C, or in salt water for more than twelve hours. This will kill any of the flatworms that are hidden from view and any eggs. It won't kill the plant.

So there we have it – suckers, munchers and accidentals: the three horsemen of the gardener's apocalypse. What do we do about them?

Mole

Wanted – for tunnelling.

Sucker or feeder – neither. Meat eater with suspected links to radical vegetarians. Could be just the wrong mammal in the wrong place at the wrong time. Under surveillance.

Favourite meal – worms and other useful soil creatures.

Where to look – underground.

Evidence – small piles of fine soil on your lawn or bed.

How to stop them – listen to Jasper Carrot's sketch 'The Mole' and follow the instructions. Alternatively, trap moles in late winter and early spring when their runs are easier to locate. When you find a run place a mole trap (available commercially) in a straight length of run within 15-20cm of the surface. Then examine trap once a day. If you haven't caught anything by the end of the fourth day, move trap to another run. There are also lots of theories about using repellants such as smelly fish and wine bottles placed in mole holes to catch the wind (the sound of which is said to irritate the moles).

What happens in nature

Or why the planet is green and we don't have to wade through honeydew swamps to get to Tesco's...

There are two reasons why the planet is green and not a barren denuded wasteland full of enormous bloated aphids and oceans of honeydew. The first is that plants have their own natural defences and the second is that pests get eaten by predators. Since plants, pests and predators have evolved together over millions of years it is no surprise that a balance has emerged between the three of them that allows them all to continue living and prevents none of them dominating at the expense of the other two. Predators need pests who need plants who need predators. All three of them need decomposers. Decomposers turn waste into humus, the non-rocky part of soil, which contains nutrients used by plants to aid growth. Of course without plants, pests and predators, decomposers would have nothing to decompose. So everyone needs everyone else.

Over 430 million years, plants have learnt how to protect themselves very well. Both through obvious physical defences – tough skin, hairy leaves, spikes, thorns, hard shells on fruit – and more discreet chemical defences, which makes them unpleasant to eat or even detrimental to those who do. Cyanide, which occurs in rose seeds, apricot, almond and black cherry stones, is one of the most obvious examples. But there are many others. Sometimes one animal's poison is another's pleasure. Ragwort, for example, is poisonous to cattle but not to the caterpillar of the cinnabar moth. Plants also protect themselves by outpacing their pests, either by becoming too big to digest or big enough to afford to give away a little bite here or there.

The bramble must be the best defended plant in Britain. It grows fast, has an incredibly tough stem, unattractive leaves and huge shark fin spikes to puncture tender tongues. Only a creature driven mad by starvation would bother having a go at that. In fact, a small fungal growth called blackberry cane spot is the only thing that will attack undeterred.

In reproductive terms plants are also first rate survivors, sometimes producing thousands of seeds per plant and distributing them over areas that can stretch to hundreds of square miles. They travel on the wind, on the legs of animals, downstream, even sometimes across oceans. Plants are not as namby-pamby as we might imagine. In fact they're far better at surviving in their natural environment than we are. Given a year in a wilderness with nothing but your own physical and mental capabilities, how would you fare?

Perhaps it is unfair to make that comparison. Homo sapiens has been re-designed for modern living and couldn't possibly be expected to perform like a contestant in some real life version of 'I'm A Celebrity Get Me Out of Here'. But in a way it is a good observation to make, for that is exactly the demand we make of our plants. In many cases, we have taken them out of their natural environment and placed them in ours, expecting them to do as well as they would in situations where millions of years of evolutionary development have given them a different set of expectations.

Plants have evolved to live in diverse environments where they can gain benefit from one another. Pests find it harder to find their victims if they are sheltered amongst plants of varying colours, shapes, tastes and scents.

The truth is pests love tidiness just as much as we do. Growing plants of the same type in rows in open fields is like laying out all your best aircraft in one place, painting them pink and handing your enemy directions to the airstrip. A good military strategist uses camouflage, subterfuge and diversity to win wars. Not just thundering big bombs.

Many pests are specific to one type or family of plants. We have already come across the cabbage white butterfly and the carrot fly in this book, but what about the blackcurrant gall midge, the box sucker (as in the hedging plant), the Chrysanthemum leaf miner. And so on… If you grow plants of the same kind in the same space without providing any barriers to movement, or the type of environment to which predators will be attracted, it will be easy for pests to move freely between plants without being threatened by their natural enemies.

Gardeners who use chemical pesticides get round this problem by spraying their pests with poisons. Organic gardeners do not have, or want, this option. For good reason… Chemical pest control is not as simple or effective as it sounds.

The Chemical Option

Of all the insects that land on a plant, only a few are there to despoil it. The rest have other things on their minds. Pollinators, predators and decomposers congregate around plants in huge numbers.

Chemical sprays seem an easy option but they do not discriminate

A lesson in diversity from indigenous tribes...

I found this quote, from E Anderson's book Plants, Man and Life, *in* The Gardener's Guide to Common-Sense Pest Control *by Olkowski and Daar, an excellent book to which all pest control addicts should refer. It describes the tropical gardens of Central American Indians he visited on a field trip in the sixties.*

'The garden was a small affair about the size of a small city lot in the United States. It was covered with a riotous growth so luxuriant and so apparently planless that any ordinary American or European visitor, accustomed to the puritanical primness of north European gardens, would have supposed (if he even chanced to realise that it was indeed a garden) that it must be a deserted one. The garden was a vegetable garden, an orchard, a medicinal garden, a dump heap and a bee yard. Plants of the same sort were so isolated from one another by intervening vegetation that pests and diseases could not readily spread from plant to plant.'

between pest and predator – the good, the bad and the ugly are wiped out without prejudice. Organic gardeners are looking to get a balance of pests and predators, so that whenever pests arrive on the scene, predators are never far behind. The organic gardener believes in biology (which to a large extent is free) rather than chemistry (which isn't). It's a better science to believe in. Populations of pests recover more quickly from chemical attack than do the predators killed in the same bout, because in almost all cases they breed more often and bring their progeny into the world at a faster and more prolific rate. A gardener without predators soon becomes more reliant on chemicals. What looks like initial victory turns out to be more like shooting oneself in the foot. With the original predators gone the pests regroup and rise again, only this time there's nothing to attack them. Except more chemicals.

Whereas pests only become resistant to predators over thousands of years of evolutionary warfare, they can quickly learn to resist attack by a specific chemical – becoming fully resistant to some chemicals in as few as forty generations. Since some pests produce five or six generations a year, a chemical can fail within a comparatively short time. This is why manufacturers have to keep on bringing out new ones.

If you think using chemicals is an easy option, think again. Not only do gardeners who use chemicals have to observe their garden just like organic gardeners do, they have to employ a whole series of time-consuming procedures including:

- selecting the correct chemical application
- selecting the brand of chemical they prefer
- equipping themselves with the tools of the trade and the right safety gear
- putting the safety gear on and taking it off, including goggles, respirator, gloves and total body coverage
- storing or disposing of unused chemicals correctly and safely out of reach of children and pets who also share the garden

But if we don't use chemicals, can we be sure that predators will turn up to do the job for us? The truth is we can't be absolutely sure that they will, not 100% of the time, in all situations and at the time we need them. This is why organic gardeners have to use other non-chemical pest control techniques too. Few organic gardeners leave it to nature entirely. We'll get on to those techniques later, but for the time being it's important to do a little trust workshop.

The main disadvantage with the pest-predator relationship is that the predators always seem to be a bit like the cavalry in those old western movies, turning up at the last moment to save the day. The pests always seem to be one step ahead of the rest of the world.

For us it is one of the misfortunes of the pest-predator relationship that predators will only appear when there is enough food to eat. This gives the impression that they're not around at all, but as sure as day follows night, predators follow prey. It is a basic evolutionary principle. In a diverse garden that hasn't been treated with chemicals predators will already be in the area, waiting for signs that the time is right to breed and attack (breed, because it is quite often their young, as well as – or rather than – the adults, that do the attacking). The important thing to remember is that there will always be a natural lag and not to be freaked out by that.

Cabbage White Butterfly

Wanted – for loitering with intent.

Sucker or feeder – feeder.

Favourite meal – could it be... But also all brassicas.

Where to look – in the air immediately above brassica plants.

Evidence – cabbage white butterflies are harmless creatures who eat nectar and pollinate our plants. However, they also lay their eggs on brassica leaves. Their eggs hatch into caterpillars and the caterpillars eat the leaves of our plants. Look for clusters of bright orange eggs and yellow and black caterpillars.

How to stop them – look at your plants frequently and remove any eggs and caterpillars you find. Encourage parastic wasps by watering plants in dry periods (wasps drink from water droplets on plants). You can grow crops under fine meshing to keep the butterflies out.

Biological control – Bacillus thuringiensis (Bt).

Knowing this helps us to make our pest control decisions scientifically rather than basing them on fear. The length of this time lag can vary from a day to a few weeks, but you will get a feel for it by monitoring how your garden usually performs. Sometimes, if the pest infestation is so severe that it looks like your plant will be permanently damaged, you will need to take action yourself. Guessing when that point has been reached is a skill, but one that can be learnt through observation.

The predators – who are they and what do they like?

The predators are a rum bunch of piratical bullies, and no mistake. Some are shrouded in mystery, concealed in shapes we ourselves fear. The eight-legged army of spiders and mites that passes across our grassy consciousness for example. Others confuse us. Who knows the difference between millipedes and centipedes, and which one is a good predator? (See below for answer.) And some we are simply dazzled by. So much so that we forget that they are predators at all. Instead we are transfixed by their beautiful bodies, elegant habits, spectacular abilities and names that conjure up feelings of great empathy, love and joy. Ladybird and dragonfly, song thrush and blue tit, frog and toad. Finally, there are those predators with which most of us are unfamiliar, that only a gardener would know about – the hoverflies, the ground and rove beetles, the slow-worm, the lacewings, the predatory bugs and the parasitic wasps. All beautiful, elegant and spectacular, but somehow absent from popular human consciousness. Where are the nursery rhymes, the fables and the fairy tales about these creatures?

Spiders

Of the spiders, not all prefer to float in their rigging. Some prefer scuttling about the forest-like stems of our little plants looking for action.

In amongst the other land armies they range about like lone samurai, viscious hunting-bayonet pincers permanently fixed and ready to pinch life away. On the whole we don't care very much for spiders, but they eat nothing but meat.

Mites

Even more mysterious to our human eyes is the predatory mite, another eight-legged wonder, but this one no greater than 1 mm long. Its favourite food? Other mites. And thrips. Those sunny-side-up suckers I talked about earlier. As thrips measure in at a whacking 2 mm long, this must make quite a lunch for the miniscule mite. You might see the event if you happened to be browsing through your plants looking for some leaf-top action, but you'll need a magnifying glass. Otherwise, most mite wrestling goes on out of sight in the top layers of soil, compost, animal manures and moss.

Centipedes

There are over 3,000 known species of centipedes and all
of them have only one pair of legs in each segment of their
elongated, articulated bodies. Millipedes, of course, have two.
Most of the 3,000 species of centipedes do not appear in
the garden but those that do hunt ferociously, using
stealth, speed and poison to kill prey. So what do
millipedes eat? Rotting food mostly, although
they have also been known to damage seedlings.

Predators we love...

And so we come to the great glorious garrison of gastronomic garden heroes, those with a taste for the peculiar and an appetite to go with it. Those
species with which we readily identify, even empathise. And that do good

things in the garden. Why we should take a liking to these creatures over others is a question the answer to which lies in the mists of time, when suspicion and sentiment ruled over science. But even now we will never love spiders like we love ladybirds. If only they looked more like they wanted a cuddle. Feeling affection for a centipede takes a lot of effort. Feeling it for a song thrush takes none. So it goes.

Perhaps if a centipede could sing it would command our attention. Or if it generated the same satisfying sound of predation as the song thrush. The instantly recognisable crack of snail shell against patio stone and concrete slab.

We humans are a funny bunch. We all know what an adult ladybird looks like, but their offspring kill more aphids. Before a ladybird larva reaches maturity it will eat 300-400 aphids. Why are we undone by the charm of the adults and not the young? Because in this case the young are ugly. Look out for them on an aphid infested stalk near you!

Water-based predators

One of the standard bits of advice in any wildlife gardening book is to build a pond. And for good reason. A pond carries a motherlode of predators. They are the marine forces every gardener needs. Perhaps the most beneficial are frogs and toads, both of which eat slugs, but dragon- and damsel-flies are predators too.

Hoverflies are also more likely to be found in gardens with ponds. They, too, are predators that seem to have slipped under the cultural radar, along with the ground and rove beetles, the slow-worm, the lacewing, the predatory bugs and the parasitic wasps. Although strictly speaking parasitic wasps are not predators at all, as they do not directly kill their prey. I want to trek on to that particular path in a moment, but before we do let's sit for a while at this rich bank of predation.

The beetles

Let's start with the beetles. 'We love you, yeah, yeah, yeah.' The beetles are one of those rare groups of insects to which we are able to show some affection even though we're not quite sure what they are, or what they are up to. Whatever they are we have a vague notion that beetles are good guys. Perhaps they have their brand leader the ladybird to thank for that.

In fact if most people were asked to name a beetle other than a ladybird they would probably go for John, Paul, George or Ringo. Unless they were gardeners! Apart from the fairly lengthy list of beetle pests there's a couple of families of good guys to mention. Both the ground (to

the left) and the rove (above) beetles are proficient hunters of pests. As their name suggests, ground beetles mostly inhabit the ground, but

56

they also hunt on leaves and flowers. Being nocturnal they're not all that easy to spot. They're quick runners, too, so any torchlight search will have to be vigilant.

Studies of their eating habits have shown them to consume a wide range of beneficial insects as well as pests, including worms, thrips, caterpillars, aphids, adult flies, spiders, slugs, the eggs of various invertebrate species and rove beetles. The fact that they eat rove beetles is not that suprising. Many predators are fairly indiscriminate about what they eat.

The slow-worm

The slow-worm is no exception to this rule, eating a mixed diet of pest and predator. Brown or silver, scaled and whip-tongued, looking every bit like a snake when it moves across the ground, this slim round creature is actually a legless lizard. During the day and in dry weather it will hide out in compost heaps, under damp stones, or in crevices in walls, but at night, or after rainfall, it will slip out of its hiding place and feed on slugs, snails, beetles and woodlice. Although they start off life as 7cm babies, by the time they reach full adulthood, slow-worms are (at 30-50cm) one of the largest garden predators we have.

Flies and bugs

Slow-worms are one of those species of animals with which we have saddled a name that not only does not describe what it does, but also puts it in with groups of creatures with which it has very little in common. We get into a similar muddle over flies and bugs. Flies and bugs are two words that are bandied about to describe any number of random invertebrates, but in the world of pest control it is important to get the taxonomy (i.e. the naming and classification of species) right. There are true flies and true bugs and, in both cases, a few species in each order are true predators.

Taxonomy: why biologists classify species into groups

There are many millions of species in the world. Scientists order them so that they can be studied with greater ease and success. Every scientist follows a system of ordering developed two centuries ago by Swedish biologist Linnaeus. Linnaeus worked out that individual species shared characteristics that allowed him to place them in larger groups (each of which he called a genus). From there he established that groups of genera (plural of genus) shared characteristics that allowed them to be placed in families, and groups of families shared characteristics that allowed them to be placed in orders. And so on through higher groups known as class, phylum and kingdom. To give you an indication of how the classification system works, turn the page for two examples, one for Homo sapiens (or man) and one for a species of moth.

You are probably familiar with the words mammalia, primate and hominidae. The word chordata means having a spinal chord. In the second column the word anthropoda means having jointed legs but no back bone.

True flies belong to the order Diptera. Which means two-winged. The order includes several families who predate on other insects (including horse-flies and robber flies) but none are as noticeable to the gardener as hover-flies (or Syrphidae – to give them their Latin name). There are two hundred and fifty species of hover-fly in Britain, and each looks slightly (and sometimes completely) different to the next. Many resemble bees or wasps, whilst others look more like houseflies. They are roughly the same length but have much less body mass. They can often be seen resting on or hovering above flowers with open heads (from which they will take nectar), or around aphid-infested plants. Both adults and young eat aphids, so look out for maggot-like larvae crawling around aphid colonies.

True bugs belong to the order Hemiptera. They have one thing in common – a piercing beak that is used for sucking the sap from plants (or blood from animals). We've already met three true bugs – shield bugs, aphids and whitefly. On the side of the predator we have water bugs such as pond skaters, damsel bugs and other individual species scattered amongst families of vegetarians.

The lacewing

On the whole true bugs play a secondary role in pest control compared to our next group – the lacewings, or Neuroptera. There are 18 species of lacewing in Britain, and all of them consume huge numbers of aphids and other small insects. This time their name is spot on, describing as it does their intricately veined, transparent and delicate wings. In this family both the adults and the children are predators, the lacewing larvae assaulting their prey with huge hollow tusks, through which they suck out their juices. These tusks set them apart from the ladybird larvae. Ladybirds have tiny devil horns – which may explain why the Italians call them the Devil's Chicken.

The parasitoids

As far as I know no one in Italy has come up with a nickname for a parasitic wasp but the Devil's Postman might be appropriate. A parasitic wasp delivers a little parcel to every victim. An egg that will grow to be a larva. Once the larva is hatched it will feed upon its 'host', keeping it alive until the larva is ready to leave home. You can see parasitic wasps in action in the garden. The action is likely to be small-scale and quick, but it is distinctive. A parasitic wasp has a needle-like tube called an ovipositor on its abdomen. Each time it lays an egg it curves its abdomen under its head, lowers itself on to the victim and punctures a hole in its victim's skin, depositing the egg inside.

Many pests have their own parasitoid wasp peculiar to their species. These wasps are known as species specific. Wasps are also stage specific, which means they prefer to lay their eggs at a specific stage of the life cycle of their victim. They have three choices – in the egg, the larva (i.e. caterpillar or grub) or direct into the adult. Either way, the egg hatches into a larva, which eats its way out of the host. Sometimes the larva of the wasp matures into an adult inside its victim and has to punch its way out. Adult aphids die this way. You see them belly up, stiff, shiny and with a hole in the side where the adult wasp has crawled out, fattened up on aphid flesh, ready to take on the world.

Parasitic creatures exist across the whole insect world and include the true fly Tachnidae, which roams around the garden making unwanted deliveries to caterpillars.

Because many of them target one species and only one species, and sometimes only one life stage, they are used extensively as a commercial biological control. Many will crop up in a garden anyway, but gardeners can 'buy them in' to tackle specific pest problems where other methods have failed, especially in a greenhouse where they are less likely to fly off to other gardens. Unlike chemical sprays they only kill their intended target and their use does not lead to the loss of other predator or harmless species. They are of course still rather unpleasant for the victim but there is nothing the gardener is doing that wouldn't happen naturally.

One of the most popular commercially available parasitoids is the slug killer Nemaslug®. This is the nematode Phasmarhabditis hermaphrodita. Nematodes are microscopic worms that burrow their way into a victim's skin. They usually hang out in damp soils, waving their tails around to detect their next victim a bit like someone waving at a passing tanker as it pushes through the ocean. If they get lucky they hitch themselves a lift, moving through the soil in a thin film of liquid to enter their host through any opening available. Once inside they develop into adult males and females and lay eggs. The eggs hatch and continue reproducing until they are forced out by competition, lack of food or the death of the host. The nematode takes a few days to kill off its carrier, ruining its appetite and starving it of food.

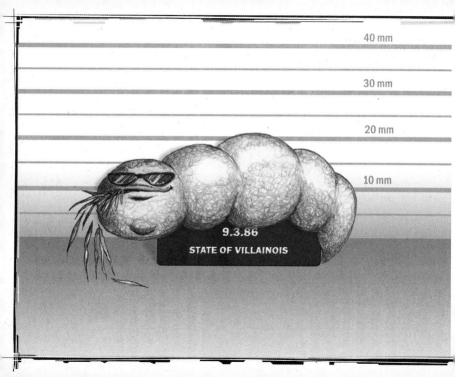

Leatherjacket

Wanted – for possession.

Sucker or feeder – feeder.

Favourite meal – grass, but also brassicas, strawberries and lettuce.

Where to look – beneath yellowing patches of lawn, where the disappearance of roots has obviously caused the grass to die. Also where starlings are probing the lawn for food. They love leatherjackets.

Evidence – it's important to find the leatherjackets before you apply any control method as similar damage can be caused by cutworms and root funghi.

How to stop them – grow strong plants in pots before planting out. On lawns larvae will come to the surface if you water infested patches heavily and place a tarpaulin or other cover on top. Once on the surface you will be able to remove them. You can also use this method on a cultivated bed if you put grass clippings underneath the cover.

Biological control – Steinernema feltiae.

And finally... Pathogens

Pathogens carry diseases between pests just as they do between humans. They have plagues just as we do. You would think that there would be nothing much the gardener could do to smite pestilence with plague, but the organic gardener has a biological weapon available – Bacillus thuringiensis (Bt). Bt was first discovered in 1911 in diseased Mediterranean flour moths. It attacked the moth with toxic protein chrystals.

Olkoswki and Daar describe the process of what actually happens to the insect unlucky enough to fall victim to this pathogen in their book, *The Gardeners' Guide to Common Sense Pest Control*:

'The components of the crystal attach to the gut wall, blocking the enzyme systems that protect the insect's gut from its own digestive juices. In a short time, holes appear in the gut wall, allowing the gut's contents to enter the insect's body cavity and bloodstream. This initial poisoning causes the insect to stop feeding and may also lead to paralysis. Then bacterial spores invade the insect's body cavity through these holes, producing septicaemia (blood poisoning) which may kill the insect immediately or may take a few days to do so.'

The Four P's

There we have it then. Predators, parasitoids and pathogens – the three p's that stop pests (the fourth p) taking over the world.

What each of the four p's have in common is their desire to come into contact with weak victims, easy targets and crowds. No one wants to work harder than they have to to get what they want and the four p's are no exception. The gardener's job is to influence the course of natural events in a way that will secure the result he or she wants. How to do this is the subject of the next section.

Part Two

Commander, soldier, defender and pacifist – which are you?

I'm going to set you a little test now. It'll enable you to work out what sort of gardener you are. Over the next three pages are three pest control questions. Answer them as honestly as you can!

Question One
If I come into my vegetable patch one morning and find some of my plants infested with aphids, do I…
a) closely observe how many aphids there are, see if there are any predators in the immediate area, jot some notes in a notebook and move on, remembering to come back tomorrow and the next day to see if there is any change?
b) squash the offending victims between finger and thumb and move on,

remembering to wipe the stains off my gloves when I get in?

c) spray organically approved derris over the entire plot just in case, remembering to order a replacement load when I get in?

d) sit and watch the aphids for hours, marvelling at the diversity of life?

Question Two

If I come into my vegetable plot one morning and find an entire row of seedlings eaten by slugs, do I…

a) check to see if there are any visual signs of slug or any other damage and make sure it is actually slugs that did the damage?

b) curse myself for not coming out in the rain the night before, with a torch and a large bucket of salty water?

c) phone up Acme Organic Pest Control Supplies immediately for five more slug traps, a roll of copper tape and several kilograms of abrasive surface material, over which I am sure sure the slugs will not venture?

d) think 'that's all right, I'll just plant some more'?

Question Three

If I wake up one winter day and start planning my next season's activities, do I…

a) check my soil quality and acidity levels, choose my seeds according to the conditions I have in my garden, read through the notes I have taken throughout the last year and clean my observation tool kit?

b) clean my scissors (the ones I use for cutting slugs in half), make sure I have enough organically approved insecticidal soap to last me through the year, buy a new pair of gloves (because the material around the thumb and finger is stained with aphid and caterpillar juice)?

c) phone up a mail order company and order fresh supplies of slug barriers, netting, fencing, cat alarms, lion dung, mole traps and an ultrasonic device that guarantees to keep giraffes away from my allotment plot?

d) find myself browsing through books on the medicinal, herbal and otherwise amazing qualities of weeds?

If you have answered 'a' to each of these questions you are showing distinct signs of being a commander; if 'b' a soldier, 'c' a defender and 'd' a pacifist.

Commanders are planners and strategists, getting the battle ground organised in advance, monitoring action as it develops and employing strategic forces when it is necessary. The commander will hold off from direct soldiering until she feels there is no other option. And when she does, she will prefer to use biological controls over other methods.

The soldier prefers to be, or is compelled by circumstance to be, in the thick of things, reacting to a situation as it develops, employing immediate force to a problem that might well have been avoided if he had more carefully planned his gardening activities.

The defender prefers to set things up in advance like the commander, but relies on man-made objects, rather than those natural forces the commander might employ, as a first line of defence. The defender expects the worst and probably gets it, perhaps because she has not taken time to work out what her plants need.

Finally, the pacifist… The pacifist is somewhat reluctant to get involved in all this warfare. While the other three are determined to plant and grow difficult crops susceptible to attack by pests, the pacifist would rather just have a garden full of plants that more or less look after themselves. Much less to think about in the long run…

Rabbit

Wanted – for anti-social behaviour.

Sucker or feeder – feeder.

Favourite meal – 'Ahh, what's up Doc'?' What's up is that each rabbit can eat a pound of vegetables a day. A family of Watership Down relocatees can demolish a garden in a couple of days.

Where to look – in your carrot patch, or pressed up against your rabbit-proof fencing like Glastonbury fans without a ticket. They feed at night, early morning or late afternoon.

Evidence – bobbing bottoms and pairs of big ears.

How to stop them – watch 'Wallace and Gromit and The Curse of the Were Rabbit' and follow the instructions. Alternatively, erect a rabbit-proof fence around either the whole garden or precious areas within it. A fence should be 1 to 1.2 metres high and be dug into the soil a further 30 centimetres and turned out away from the garden. Use a mesh size of 2.5 to 3cm. Some plants are less attractive to rabbits. See Janet Thompson's book 'Common Garden Enemies' and 'Living with the Enemy'.

The commander

Plants need light, air, water and nutrients from the soil to grow. They also need shelter from the wind, protection from frost and the right amount of warmth at the right time of year. They need to be grown in soils that contain the right level of acidity or alkalinity and the right levels of fertility. Furthermore, they also need to be grown in soils that contain the right amount of moisture and are in fact of the right type. Depending on the species of plant they are, they may also need to be planted between groups of plants amongst which they will thrive. If we understand all these things and get them right, then our plants will do well. If we want our plants to do brilliantly we may have to prune them, support them to stop them blowing over in the wind, remove parts that have become diseased and remedy any nutrient deficiencies that arise along the way. To do all these things we need to know a lot about our garden – where the wind blows in, where the frost settles, where the sun falls on the garden, how the water drains through the soil and so on. We need to take measurements with pH and soil fertility kits. We need to add compost or muck when it is important to do so. We need to remove weeds when they are likely to strangle our plants or take moisture out of the soil. In short we need to practise good garden care.

Any commander moving into a garden for the first time will spend a good year getting to know it: monitoring how the garden changes over twelve months, getting soil tests done (kits are available from most mail order companies and garden centres – see directory, page 115), identifying what she might consider to be any weaknesses in the garden, establishing a composting regime for the garden and kitchen waste, fencing off any areas that might be susceptible to attack by larger pests such as rabbits, sheep or deer and starting to think about which plants she would like to grow there.

A commander does not necessarily shy away from growing plants that are likely to be vulnerable to attack from pests, but she will make careful decisions before buying any. Some seeds are bred for their resistance to pests, diseases and deficiencies. Where possible a commander selects seeds carefully, choosing those which are likely to perform better in her garden. Many plants are more vulnerable to attack when they are very young. The commander assesses which plants suffer most when planted directly in the soil and elects to grow some inside in pots – only transplanting them out when they reach a more mature state. When buying a plant the commander also checks whether there are any signs of pest infestation before bringing it into the garden and removes any pests she finds.

I have already talked at length about creating abundant diversity in a garden and a good commander will choose a wide selection of plants to populate the garden. If she is growing vegetables she will practise a four year rotation, to stop soils becoming infested with pests particular to one of the four main groups of vegetable species. In amongst the vegetables she is likely to plant flowers to attract a variety of insects and allow some of their vegetables to flower – especially chicory and parsnips which have abundant nectar and beautiful flowers. She will want to grow a mixture of open and flat flowers for beetles and hover-flies, and tubular and harder to access flowers for large bees and long-tongued insects. She will also want to make sure there's something in flower all season, grow plants with a long flowering season and avoid those varieties of flowers (such as double blooms) which have been highly modified by plant breeders. These tend to have less nectar than older varieties, because they have been bred for other qualities such as shape, colour and form. Sometimes the 'design' of these newer flower varieties is so complicated that pollinators can't get at the nectar.

A commander will observe her garden well. She will have a surveillance policy, going out regularly to check on the health of her plants – seeing what troop activities they can find. If there are pest problems she will keep records of what damage occurred, which pests were evident, what conditions they thrived in and think about what might have caused the outbreak. To test the strength of the predator population she may leave some plants lightly infested with insect pests to see if natural predators move in. A few tools are essential for this task – a notebook to keep records, to which she can refer later if subsequent outbreaks occur; a selection of containers to collect samples; a hand lens to take a closer look and some night visioning equipment to seek out nocturnal pests and predators. A hand torch will suffice but an adjustable head torch is better.

Keeping records is not as time consuming as it sounds and may save time and money in the long run. By learning how the predator community works she is more likely to resist intervening with sprays or other time consuming methods of control. Record keepers are more likely to identify the correct pest and to identify the true cause of an outbreak when it occurs, be it bad gardening practice, climatic variations or other external events beyond the control of the gardener.

Sometimes the commander will be able to identify the cause of her problems as being her own horticultural practice. For example, many pests like to launch attacks from clumps of nearby weeds. This is particularly the case with slugs and snails. Keeping the beds tidy will reduce pest damage.

Commanders should also be more responsive to the needs of predators. Parasitic wasps, for example, like to drink from water droplets on plants. Ensuring plants are sprinkled on dry days will provide a much needed water source.

Nematodes, parasitic wasps and other parasitoids target specific pests and are commercially available. In fact, 400 pests have been found to be susceptible to parasitoids or parasites, although not all these have appeared on the market. Those that do are described in the box below. They are safe, require no unusual or expensive equipment, can be delivered through the post and can be used in the garden without fear of causing damage to non-target species. The commander makes use of them strategically, to deal with outbreaks of pests when the predator pest balance fails, and when direct soldiering or defending is not an option.

Predators and parasitoids by post

Most commercially available predators and parasitoids are bred in laboratory conditions and sent out to people on demand. They are best used on the day of arrival. Manufacturers recommend you only order them when you've seen the pest in your garden and not before. This is because many biological controls need very specific conditions in which to operate and may only live for a short period of time. For example, the predator of the red spider mite is another mite Phytosielius. It is for use in the confines of the greenhouse and will only operate if the daytime minimum temperature does not fall below 20°C or rise above 30°C.

On a very hot day you may have to vent your greenhouse or use shading to keep the temperature right. At night the temperature must remain above 16°C. Other controls are less fussy. The vine weevil control – the nematode Steinernema kraussei – functions down to temperatures as low as 5°C. The pests come in a packet with full instructions, but if you're not sure about anything talk to the supplier before you order and make sure the time and conditions are right for use. As each packet costs £14 you should avoid costly mistakes if you can. Identify your pest correctly, check conditions are right for use and order so they arrive on a day you know you'll be able to apply them. Some controls are specifically for use in greenhouses and others for use outdoors, some will last a season, others a week or so. Application is straightforward... Many are applied with water in a watering can; others are applied directly with a little shake of the packet. Those supplied in tubes fly or crawl out when you take the lid off. It's all quite simple. You can also buy homes for predators – lacewing and ladybird hotels being the most common. These are designed to recreate preferred nesting conditions, but do not always attract residents, especially if they are placed incorrectly. You can also buy a ladybird kit and grow eggs from the larvae stage through to fully fledged adults. Names and addresses of suppliers are in the directory on page 115.

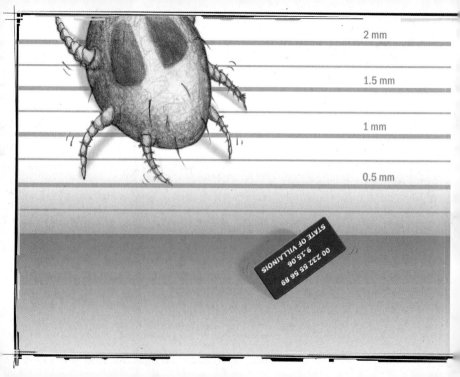

2 mm

1.5 mm

1 mm

0.5 mm

STATE OF VILLAINOIS
9.15.06
00 232 55 56 89

Glasshouse red spider mite

Wanted – for burglary.

Sucker or feeder – sucker.

Favourite meal – not fussy, a wide range of plants

Where to look – although they do eat al fresco in very hot dry summers they prefer dining à la carte in glasshouses, conservatories or the house proper. On the undersides of leaves, especially between June and September. In winter they hibernate in cracks and crevices, leaf litter and garden canes.

Evidence – leaves speckle, bronze and eventually wither. Red spider mites produce a fine webbing. The mites themselves can be seen through a magnifying glass. They are only red during autumn and winter. The rest of the year they are pale green/yellow with two dark spots.

How to stop them – use a high pressure hose in spring to clear out cracks and crevices. Get rid of badly infected plants. Don't let plants get too big for their pots or overcrowded. Spray infested plants with a fine mist, twice daily.

Biological control – Phytoseiulus persimilis.

The soldier

There's a streak of Dad's Army's Corporal Jones in all of us. Especially if there's a slug involved. Where the commander holds back, the soldier is always ready to fix bayonets, even if the words 'Don't panic' are hanging on his lips as he does so. The soldier lacks the overall strategic view of the commander and prefers to wage war directly, squeezing, crushing, throwing and poisoning pests himself rather than leaving it to some namby pamby predator, which may or may not be present.

Taken to extremes, the soldier who has not prepared his garden as a commander would finds himself in perpetual combat. Trapped by his own lack of preparation and knowledge and with very few natural predators to help him along, he finds himself fighting enemy forces that are stronger than they should be, and using more firepower than is absolutely necessary. The armoury at his disposal, his own hands, his pest control tools and of course pesticides, are constantly engaged.

You would think that the benefits of being more like a commander would be evident to the struggling squaddie, but there is a lot to be said for soldiering. A soldier gets satisfaction from believing he's on top of things, even if he isn't. A soldier is familiar with the enemy and the state of play in his garden. A soldier removes pests from the battlefield. Of course the more pests he removes himself the less interest there is for natural predators, but the soldier is unaware of such subtleties. He's not that interested in note-taking either. The soldier is more physical than cerebral. He just likes to get on with the job. Even if getting on with the job means spending considerably more time controlling pests than he would if he let predators do the job for him.

In the end the soldier believes he is the only one capable of doing the job that needs to be done. He would be uncomfortable with the idea of a pest-predator time lag and would hate having to wait a few days to see if natural predators turn up. Moreover, a soldier would wonder at the gall of companies selling predators and parasitoids. After all they're so small you can't even see them in action, let alone know if they work. And sometimes when you unwrap the packet it looks like you've paid £15 for a small bag of sawdust. The soldier prefers large containers of pesticides, boot heels, fingers and thumbs, water jets, knives (which they name 'Slugger'), scissors with sharpened edges. Real things with results you can see with your own eyes.

What then are the tools available to the soldier and when should he use them? The soldier likes hand-to-hand combat, especially as he is considerably larger than anything he is likely to fight. When he can he will remove insects by hand and in some way destroy them, either by removing them from their food source, crushing them, or, in the case of the slug, committing endless acts of mutilation upon them. Light infestations of most of the smaller pests can be crushed between finger and thumb. Those that are a little bigger can be flattened under foot, or using the back of a trowel. Some nocturnal pests like to find shelter during the day and the soldier will facilitate the removal of pests by laying deliberate shelter traps. This is particularly the case with slugs, which like to shelter under slabs of wood, stone, old plant pots, and in amongst harvested comfrey leaves.

If a plant is heavily infested, depending on the pest, a soldier has a number of other options available to him. The flea beetle (which attacks brassicas) can be removed using a piece of board smothered with grease. The board is drawn along the tops of infested plants, not so heavily as to damage them but just enough to dislodge the pests. The flea beetle, as its name suggests, prefers to jump away from trouble. It jumps upwards on to the board and gets stuck there. The method isn't foolproof. It's messy, and many beetles will miss the board.

Some of the less mobile pests (such as aphids) can be removed with a fine jet of water. Looking for them, and then directing the water at them in their hiding places, is probably the hardest part of the deal. Once dislodged they fall easily. Beware of protective ants though. Holding the leaf, spraying and avoiding ant bites all at the same time can be a tricky business. This sort of treatment might need consistent renewal too as it is not likely to kill off entire colonies of pests. Revisit plants regularly to see if they're back.

As a last resort organic soldiers can use a range of pesticides that have been approved by the Soil Association (the governing body of the organic movement in the UK). These are not species specific, and some can kill predators as well as pests. They can also be dangerous if used incorrectly and full protective clothing must be worn when spraying. Nevertheless, as an alternative to conventional chemical pesticides, and as a last resort, they can be used as a less harmful option than conventional chemicals.

Approved pesticides and their uses

- *Derris* – used against greenfly, blackfly and other aphids; caterpillars; flea beetle; raspberry beetle; sawfly larvae (can harm ladybirds, lacewings and parasitic wasps)
- *Pyrethrum* – greenfly, blackfly and other aphids (can harm beneficials)
- *Insecticidal soap* – greenfly, blackfly and other aphids; whitefly; red spider mite; soft scale; rose slugworm (makes the pests slip off rather than harming them)
- *Rapeseed oil* – greenfly, blackfly and other aphids; whitefly; thrips; scale; red spider mite (not to be used on fuschias, begonias and seedlings, because it can damage their leaves)
- *Bordeaux mixture* – apple scab; peach leaf curl; potato blight (harmful to fish, livestock and worms)
- *Sulphur* – powdery mildew and rose black spot (can harm predatory mites; not to be used on young apples and gooseberries)
- *Bacillus thuringiensis (Bt)* – used on caterpillars

Derris, pyrethrum, insecticidal soap and rapeseed oil are all extracted from plant material. Bordeaux mixture is a compound of copper and sulphur (both of which are naturally occurring minerals) and Bt is a bacterial spore. These natural materials are used in preference to chemical compounds created in the lab because of their favourably low toxicity levels. However, they are constantly under review and the horticultural organisation Garden Organic believes that the use of copper products and derris in organic systems will be banned in the next few years. Many people make pesticides at home out of plant material but this practice is illegal. Despite all this no pesticides approved for use in organic systems have ever been shown to produce the same amount of damage to wildlife and humans as chemical pesticides, most notably DDT.

The defender

The defender is a cross between a commander and a soldier. She doesn't want to rely on natural predators but, rather than reacting to situations as they arise, makes plenty of preparations before hostilities commence. She is a pre-emptive defender, setting up traps and barriers right at the start of the season, and ensuring they are operational throughout the whole campaign. Slug traps are topped up with beer, pheromone traps kept scented, grease bands slick, copper rings maintained. The defender expects the worst, and with so many traps around usually finds plenty of evidence that that's what she got.

There is a daily ritual to the defender's tour of duty: a beat. Having established strategic places to position her traps, the defender visits them each day and removes the contents. Inside some she will find strange, beery, meaty stews of slugs, snails and beetles. In others there will be greased cards heavy with a mixed grill of flying insects, sticky and hot. In both cases there will be collateral damage, predators that have tasted their last meal.

There is something altogether random about a trap. Although they are usually filled with substances that pests find attractive, there are no guarantees that pests will make their way there in an orderly fashion. Like any other pest control measure they are not foolproof. Even if the defender finds her traps filled every morning it does not necessarily mean that she has protected her plants, particularly if there is evidence that the traps are capturing predators as well as pests. What she will have done is reduce the amount of life in her garden. On balance she will have to hope the net effect is positive.

Barriers are altogether more reliable and are generally used in a much more targeted way. The first thing any defender will do is wrap her garden up with fencing, making sure all sides have been shielded from large pests like sheep, deer and rabbits. Each of these pests has a slightly different aptitude for jumping over or crawling under fences, so the defender has to fence to suit the type(s) of pests she finds in her area. Sheep fencing is the easiest – a simple metre high, square pattern wire fence will suffice. Deer fences will have to be higher – perhaps up to two metres. Rabbits will go under and through sheep fencing. To keep out burrowers you need to dig a 2.5cm (1 inch) wire mesh fencing material one foot under the ground, bending the lower 15cm (6 inches) outwards (i.e. away from the garden).

Once the whole garden is protected from mammals the defender has to assess the danger from other classes of species. Damage caused by birds, insects and other invertebrates can be prevented, in certain circumstances, by the use of barriers. Fruit can be caged off with wire mesh or protected by a single layer of horticultural fleece (a lightweight fabric that can be easily rested on fruit without damaging it). Horticultural fleece can also be used to keep pigeons, cabbage butterflies, cabbage root fly and flea beetles away from brassicas, and carrot fly from carrots. In each case the fleece is either placed directly on top of the crop or around a frame bought or created for the purpose. The only drawback with horticultural fleece is that it does reduce air circulation and light penetration (both essential for plant health). Prolonged use beyond the early stages of plant growth can provide ideal conditions for slugs and fungal pathogens to proliferate. A more appropriate solution is insect mesh (a 1.5mm woven square net). This allows maximum penetration of light and air without letting the insects in.

For most pests you have to cover the whole crop but in the case of carrot fly a simple 75cm high mesh fence will act as a barrier. Carrot fly doesn't venture above this height so the fence stops the fly getting into the carrot patch, whilst also taking the appealing whiff of carrot upwards to the sky. Cabbage root fly can also be prevented by placing a 10cm diameter fabric collar around the stems of brassica seedlings. This prevents the female flies from laying their eggs in the soil; instead they will lay them

on the collar, where they will dry up before hatching.

The pest most likely to face a barrier is the slug. Prolonged experimentation by the gardening community has led to a potential minefield of alternative solutions for preventing slugs from making the perilous journey towards your plants. I won't bore you with them all here (OK, they're in the box below, for those of you who really want to know) but it's worth pointing out that with most of them there is absolutely no scientific proof that they work.

One of the most common is the copper band. Drawn around pots, the copper gives traversing slugs a mild electric shock. They recoil and head off somewhere else. The use of protective bands is quite commonplace in gardening. Bands of grease placed around pots will prevent earwigs, ants and adult vine weevils making it on to plants. Bands of grease placed around the trunks of fruit trees will prevent the wingless winter moth and other related species of moth climbing to lay eggs.

Carrot fly

Wanted – for low flying.

Sucker or feeder – feeder (of the tunnelling variety).

Favourite meal – umm, I wonder...

Where to look – around and in the roots of carrots and related plants such as parsley, parsnip and celery.

Evidence – the adult carrot fly: it is easier to prevent the adult getting near your plants than it is to detect and prevent the young maggots that actually cause the damage. They tunnel the roots, causing the leaves to redden and stunting growth. You can often spot the eggs of the maggots in small clusters near the plants. Remove any you find.

How to stop them – carrot fly doesn't travel above thirty inches from the ground, so you can protect your crops with a fine mesh fence... Or grow crops in high raised beds... Delay sowing until June to avoid early carrot fly and avoid uneccessary thinning when plants are mature. The thinning of plants tends to release an aroma which is very attractive to the carrot fly.

Slug barriers suggested by participants in CAT's Bug the Slug Campaign (as featured hilariously in *The Little Book of Slugs*)

Woodchip/sawdust; ash; the shells of brazils, walnuts, pistachios, sweet chestnut and/or eggs; slate/gravel chips; recycled glass chippings and other commercial materials, pine cones, sand, sheep's fleece; cocoa shell and other mulches; Vaseline; grease; Marmite or yeast extract on stems or around pots; copper rings/wire; electric fence; moats (sometimes called a butcombe box); plastic bottles.

The pacifist

There is one sure-fire way to avoid getting stressed by pests. Choose plants that pests don't like. There is nothing in the rule-book to say that we have to choose the hardest plants to grow. There are plenty of amazing plants that aren't particularly bothered by pests. Why don't we grow these?

The biggest problem you are likely to face in any unprotected garden is an invasion from mammals – in particular sheep and rabbits. As far as I know there are no conclusive lists of plants sheep won't eat (although we could start with brambles, bracken, azalea, rhododrendon and Japanese knotweed), so the basic requirement of any garden is a sound fence. But beyond that there are plenty of options. If you're troubled by rabbits try Janet Thomson's list of '105 Plants Which Rabbits Tend To Ignore' in her little book *Common Garden Enemies*.

After the mammals, the mollusc will most likely be your next biggest problem (perhaps more so in the wetter regions of the UK). The RHS receives more queries about slugs than any other pest. When CAT conducted its Bug the Slug survey, it found that some people had given up growing plants that slugs liked because it was too time-consuming to be worth the effort restraining them. Instead they switched to plants that they enjoyed but the slugs did not, of which there were many fantastic species (some of which are listed in *The Little Book of Slugs* or at www.cat.org.uk/ihateslugs).

Thereafter, most pest problems are caused by insects and birds, and many plants are not affected by either, at least not to the extent that it matters visually or materially. A pacifist avoids plants that are particularly susceptible to pest problems, such as brassicas, and sticks to those that are easy to manage. Not necessarily because he has any moral qualms about pest control but perhaps because he simply does not have the time or interest to get involved with them.

Wildflowers such as foxgloves, columbine, ox-eye daisy, Cambrian poppy, cowslip and red campion have a high tolerance of pests, and are all wonderfully attractive and beneficial plants that are easy to grow in the right conditions. Any wildlife organisation will furnish you with lists of plants that are highly beneficial for wildlife and have a high tolerance of attack by pests (see directory for contacts and websites). Likewise, many herbs are less likely to be affected by pests than other fruit and vegetable crops, and are equally useful in the kitchen.

The ultimate pacifist's garden is probably the edible forest garden, a system inspired by some of the indigenous gardens I described earlier, but adapted for our climate by Robert Hart and others (download a tipsheet from www.cat.org.uk/catpubs). The forest garden models itself on the native English woodland – having seven layers of growth that work together to reduce pest problems and increase plant health. If we want a model for a low pest garden then the English woodland is a good place to start. It maintains itself without much interference from us, produces useful food and materials, and is extremely beneficial for wildlife.

If you want to get away from traditional pest control worries try something different.

I've had lots of fun writing this book, but working out what kind of person you are, and what kind of person you would like to become, is a serious business. In reality, gardeners need to occupy the mental space of each of the four types of person described here at different times. The gardeners who get the most sleep at night are those who know when to wear the right hat. The last thing you want is a garden that torments you with troubles. Gardening is supposed to be a relaxing, peaceful pastime and a garden is a place to get away from life's stresses. The best result you can hope to achieve is to set things up so that they work well almost all the time. Then you can react to those few problems that do arise,

sensitively and with care for our natural environment.
Best wishes and happy gardening!

Directory

Bibliography and further reading

Complete British Insects, Michael Chinery, Collins, 2005

Common Garden Enemies, Janet Thompson, self published, 2000

Curious Incidents in the Garden at Night-time, Allan Shepherd, CAT Publications, 2005

Ecology for Gardeners, Carroll and Salt, Timber Press, 2004

Forest Gardening, Robert Hart, Green Books, 1996

HDRA Encyclopedia of Organic Gardening, Pauline Pears, Dorling Kindersley, 2005

How to Make a Forest Garden, Patrick Whitefield, Permanent Publications, 1996

No Nettles Required, Ken Thompson, Eden Project Books, 2006
Natural Enemies Handbook: The Illustrated Guide to Biological Pest Control, Mary Louise Flint, University of California Press, 1999
Organic Gardening Magazine, August 2006
Pests and Diseases, Pippa Greenwood and Andrew Halstead, RHS and Dorling Kindersley, 1997
Pests: How to Control Them on Fruit and Vegetables, Pauline Pears, Search Press, 2006
The Encylopedia of Insects and Invertebrates, Burton and Burton, Silverdale Books, 2002
The Gardener's Guide to Common Sense Pest Control, Olkowski, Olkowski and Daar, The Taunton Press, 1995
The Little Book of Slugs, Shepherd and Gallant, CAT Publications, 2002
The Little Book of Garden Heroes, Allan Shepherd, CAT Publications, 2004

War and Nature: Fighting Humans and Insects with Chemicals from World War I to Silent Spring, Edmund Russell, Cambridge University Press, 2001

Weeds: Friend or Foe, Sally Roth, Carroll and Brown, 2002

Wildlife Gardening for Everyone, RHS and The Wildlife Trusts, Think Books, 2006

Useful websites

www.cat.org.uk/ihateslugs
www.rhs.org.uk
www.gardenorganic.org.uk
www.wildaboutgardens.org
www.dgsgardening.btinternet.co.uk/insects.htm
   (excellent photo reference for identifying friends and foes)
www.pan-uk.org (advice and information about the use of pesticides)

Mail order pest control

Centre for Alternative Technology Mail Order,
Machynlleth, Powys, SY20 9AZ; 01654 705959; www.cat.org.uk
Just-Green Ltd, Unit 14 Springfield Road, Springfield Business Park,
Burnham on Crouch, Essex, CMO 8UA;
01621 785088; www.just-green.com
The Organic Gardening Catalogue, Riverdene Business Park,
Molesey Road, Hersham, Surrey, KT12 4RG;
0845 130 1304; www.organiccatalog.com
Wiggly Wigglers, Lower Blakemere Farm, Blakemere,
Herefordshire, HR2 9PX; 01981 500391; www.wigglywigglers.co.uk

Organisations

Centre for Alternative Technology, Machynlleth, Powys, SY20 9AZ;
01654 705950; www.cat.org.uk

Garden Organic, Ryton Organic Gardens, Coventry,
Warwickshire, CV8 3LG; 024 7630 3517; www.gardenorganic.org.uk

Pesticides Action Network, Development House, 56-64 Leonard Street,
London, EC2A 4JX; 020 7065 0905; www.pan-uk.org

RHS, 80 Vincent Square, London, SW1P 2PE;
0845 260 5000; www.rhs.org.uk

The Wildlife Trusts, The Kiln, Waterside, Mather Road, Newark,
Nottinghamshire, NG24 1WT; 0870 0367711; www.wildlifetrusts.org